SIMPLY SOUTHERN

NEWNAN JUNIOR SERVICE LEAGUE

Simply Southern

Published by Newnan Junior Service League, Inc.
P.O. Box 1433
Newnan, Georgia 30264

Library of Congress Control Number:
2007940966
ISBN: 978-0-9611002-3-0

Art Director and Book Design: Starletta Polster
Project Editor: Mary Spotswood Box

Edited, Designed, and Manufactured by
Favorite Recipes® Press
An imprint of
FRP
P. O. Box 305142
Nashville, Tennessee 37230
800-358-0560

Printed in the United States of America
First Printing: 2008
7,500 copies

The Newnan Junior Service League (NJSL) is an organization of women committed to enhancing the quality of life in our community through dedicated service, volunteerism, and leadership.

Table of Contents

Foreword

The members of the Newnan Junior Service League hope you enjoy these dishes as much as we do! Each of the recipes comes from our members, friends, and family, as well as favorite restaurants in Newnan, Georgia. *Simply Southern* contains simple, delicious recipes from our Southern roots, as well as new favorites that draw their influences from around the globe. We hope you love turning our new recipes into your old favorites.

Thank you,

Julie Hoffman

Cookbook Chairman

Newnan Junior Service League

ACTIVE MEMBERS 2006–2007

Tisa Allen
Reynie Banks
Kristin Barron
Lora Beck
Alicia Bohannon
Tabitha Boone
Alexis Brooks
Allison Bryant
Jenny Bryant
Cindy Burkhart
Betsy Burnette
Carol Cantrell
Abigail Cole
Julia Crye
Rebecca Durham
Holly Etheridge
Kelley Finger*
Melissa Griffis
Jessica Guarnera
Beth Headley*
Julie Hoffman*
Ashley Horne
Celia Huey*
Lisa Jennings*
Jennifer Jones
Jennifer Lichty*
Charlotte Lunsford*
Lesleigh MacNabb
Jennifer McKinnon
Jill Meeker
JJ Moody
Ericka Morgan
Tina Neely
Patricia Palmer
Brannan Pass
Christine Rice
Rachel Rice
Ashley Roberts
Lindsay Robison
Candice Sears
Corrie Sears
Brooke Smith*
Christy Stoffle
Lindsay Thompson*
Michelle Ward
Teresa Ward
Kallie Zollman

**Cookbook Committee*

Around Town

André's Off the Square

BRAISED LAMB SHANK

SERVES 4

4 lamb shanks
1 tablespoon kosher salt or sea salt
1 tablespoon pepper
1 cup chopped onion
1 cup chopped carrots
1 cup chopped celery
1 tablespoon finely chopped garlic
1 cup balsamic vinegar
3 quarts lamb stock, beef stock or veal stock
Fresh rosemary

Sprinkle the lamb with the salt and pepper. Roast at 425 to 450 degrees in a roasting pan or broil on High 6 inches from the heat source on a rack in a broiler pan until brown. Sauté the onion, carrots and celery in a large saucepan until tender. Stir in the garlic. Add the vinegar. Cook until the pan is dry, stirring constantly and scraping up any brown bits from the bottom of the saucepan. Add the lamb, stock and rosemary. Bring to a simmer. Simmer for 3 to 4 hours or until the meat is tender and falling off the bones.

Golden's on the Square

SWEET POTATO SOUFFLE

SERVES 8

2 pounds sweet potatoes, peeled
4 eggs, beaten
2 cups packed brown sugar
1 cup granulated sugar
1/2 cup (1 stick) butter
4 ounces pecans, chopped
2 teaspoons vanilla extract
Cinnamon to taste

Combine the sweet potatoes with enough water to cover in a large saucepan. Bring to a boil. Boil until tender; drain. Beat the sweet potatoes in a mixing bowl until smooth and fluffy. Add the eggs, brown sugar, granulated sugar, butter, pecans and vanilla; beat well. Spoon into a large soufflé dish and sprinkle with cinnamon. Bake at 350 degrees for 1 hour or until the center is set and the top is golden brown.

Mama Lucia's

LINGUINE ALLA VONGOLE

SERVES 6

1/4 cup chopped garlic
1/4 cup minced carrots
1/4 cup minced celery
Pinch of crushed red pepper
1/4 cup extra-virgin olive oil
1 cup dry white wine
1 tablespoon chopped fresh oregano
2 pounds baby clams with liquid
1/2 teaspoon salt
1 tablespoon fresh lemon juice
2 tablespoons chopped fresh parsley
16 ounces linguine pasta, cooked
1/4 cup extra-virgin olive oil

Sauté the garlic, carrots, celery and crushed red pepper in 1/4 cup olive oil in a skillet for 2 minutes. Add the wine and oregano. Cook until the wine reduces by half. Stir in the undrained clams, salt, lemon juice and parsley. Cook until the clams are tender. Add the pasta and 1/4 cup olive oil; toss to coat. Bring to a simmer. Serve immediately.

The Redneck Gourmet

REDNECK GREEK PASTA

SERVES 6 TO 8

Add sautéed chicken and you have a great main course. Add a green salad and delicious bread and you have a great meal that is always a favorite!

16 ounces penne pasta or spaghetti pasta
Salt to taste
Olive oil (do not use extra-virgin)
1 cup black olives, coarsely chopped
4 ounces good-quality feta cheese, crumbled
1/2 cup (2 ounces) grated Parmesan cheese
1 tablespoon Good Seasons Italian salad dressing mix, or to taste
Red wine vinegar to taste

Cook the pasta in boiling salted water in a large saucepan for 10 to 12 minutes or until al dente. Drain and rinse with cold water. Toss with a small amount of olive oil in a large bowl. Add the olives, feta cheese, Parmesan cheese, salad dressing mix and vinegar; toss to coat.

Ten East Washington

GEORGE'S PENNE PASTA

SERVES 4

2 tablespoons chopped garlic
1/4 cup olive oil
2 cups chopped tomatoes
1/4 cup vodka
2 cups heavy cream
2 tablespoons unsalted butter
2 tablespoons chopped fresh tarragon
12 ounces penne pasta
2 cups (8 ounces) grated Parmesan cheese
Salt and pepper to taste

Sauté the garlic in the olive oil in a large skillet over medium-high heat for 30 seconds. Add the tomatoes and bring to a simmer. Stir in the vodka, cream, butter and tarragon. Simmer for 5 to 7 minutes or until the mixture reduces by half, stirring frequently. Cook the pasta according to the package directions until al dente; drain. Add the pasta and cheese to the warm sauce; toss to coat. Season with salt and pepper. Garnish with additional chopped fresh tarragon or chopped fresh parsley.

FINE DINING

JJ Moody

WARM CHUTNEY SPINACH SALAD

SERVES 6

2 tablespoons butter
$1^1/_2$ cups coarsely chopped pecans
1 teaspoon salt
1 teaspoon pepper
12 ounces baby spinach
6 slices bacon, crisp-cooked and crumbled
1 cup dried cranberries
2 hard-cooked eggs, finely chopped
Warm Chutney Dressing (page 14)

Melt the butter in a nonstick sauté pan over medium heat. Add the pecans and cook for 2 minutes or until toasted, stirring constantly. Remove from the heat and add the salt and pepper; toss to coat. Drain on paper towels. Combine the pecans, spinach, bacon, cranberries and eggs in a bowl. Add the desired amount of warm dressing and toss to coat. Serve immediately.

WARM CHUTNEY DRESSING

MAKES 1 CUP

6 tablespoons balsamic vinegar
$^{1}/_{3}$ cup mango chutney
2 tablespoons Dijon mustard
2 garlic cloves, minced
$^{1}/_{4}$ cup olive oil

Combine the vinegar, chutney, Dijon mustard and garlic in a saucepan. Cook over medium heat for 3 minutes, stirring constantly. Add the olive oil in a thin stream, stirring constantly until combined. Cook for 1 minute. Serve immediately.

It is not necessary to cook the dressing if making ahead. Combine all ingredients in a microwave-safe container and mix well. Chill, covered, until ready to use. Microwave for 20 seconds or until warm just before serving.

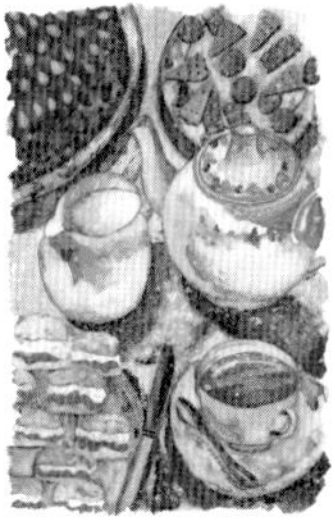

Robyn Ridgeway

FLANK STEAK

SERVES 4 TO 6

- 1/4 cup vegetable oil
- 2 tablespoons lemon juice
- 2 tablespoons soy sauce
- 2 tablespoons finely chopped onion
- 1 tablespoon meat tenderizer
- 1 garlic clove, crushed
- 1 teaspoon pepper
- 1 teaspoon celery salt
- 1 (3-pound) flank steak
- Barbecue Sauce (page 16)

Combine the oil, lemon juice, soy sauce, onion, meat tenderizer, garlic, pepper and celery salt in a sealable plastic bag; mix well. Pierce the flank steak five or six times with a fork on each side. Place the steak in the marinade and seal the bag. Chill for 6 to 10 hours. Drain, discarding the marinade. Grill the flank steak on a grill rack to desired degree of doneness. Serve Barbecue Sauce on the side.

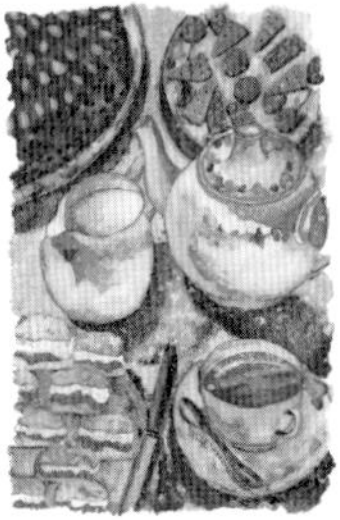

BARBECUE SAUCE

MAKES ABOUT 10 CUPS

4 cups white vinegar
2 cups prepared mustard
1 lemon, thinly sliced
1/2 (10-ounce) bottle Worcestershire sauce
2 (12-ounce) bottles chili sauce
Salt and black pepper to taste
Cayenne pepper to taste (optional)

Bring the vinegar to a boil in a saucepan. Boil for 2 minutes. Remove from the heat and add the mustard; whisk until smooth. Stir in the lemon slices, Worcestershire sauce, chili sauce, salt, black pepper and cayenne pepper. Keep warm until serving time. Discard the lemon slices before serving.

Courtenay Lee

CARROT SOUFFLE

SERVES 8

1 pound carrots, cooked
1/2 cup (1 stick) butter, melted
3 eggs, lightly beaten
1 cup sugar
2 tablespoons all-purpose flour
1 teaspoon baking powder
1 teaspoon vanilla extract

Process the carrots in a food processor until smooth. Add the butter gradually, processing constantly until smooth. Add the eggs, sugar, flour, baking powder and vanilla. Process until smooth. Spoon the mixture into a 1-quart baking dish. Bake at 350 degrees for 45 minutes. This recipe may be made a day ahead and may be doubled. If doubling the recipe, increase the amount of sugar to slightly more than a cup.

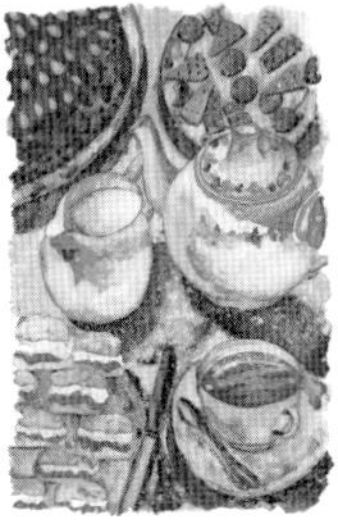

Candice Sears

CREME FRAICHE MASHED POTATOES

SERVES 8

2 cups heavy whipping cream
1 cup sour cream
1 head garlic
Olive oil
3 pounds small red potatoes
8 ounces cream cheese, softened
1/4 cup (1/2 stick) butter, softened
1/2 teaspoon salt
1/2 teaspoon pepper
1/4 cup finely chopped green onions
1 tablespoon chopped fresh chives

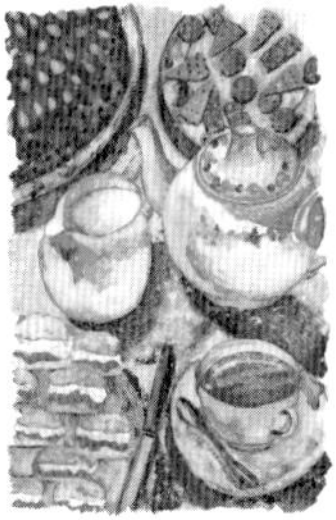

Combine the whipping cream and sour cream in a bowl and mix well. Cover tightly with plastic wrap and let the crème fraîche stand at room temperature for 24 hours; mix well. Chill, covered, for 5 hours. Remove the top one-fourth of the head of garlic. Drizzle with olive oil and wrap tightly in foil. Bake at 400 degrees for 40 minutes. Let stand until cool. Squeeze the cloves from the bulb and mince the cloves.

Peel the potatoes and cut into halves. Combine the potatoes with enough water to cover in a large saucepan. Bring to a boil. Boil until tender; drain. Combine the potatoes, half of the crème fraîche, the cream cheese, butter, 1 tablespoon of the garlic, the salt and pepper in a mixing bowl. Beat until smooth. Stir in the green onions. Spoon the mixture into a lightly greased 2-quart baking dish and smooth the top. Spread the remaining crème fraîche evenly over the top. Sprinkle with the chives. Bake at 350 degrees for 15 to 20 minutes or until the potatoes are heated through.

Purchased crème fraîche and chopped roasted garlic may be substituted.

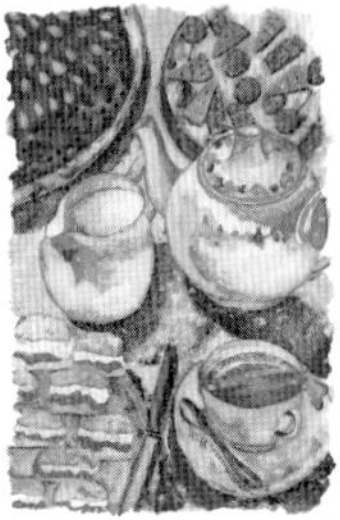

Annemarie Grubbs

ASPARAGUS SQUASH CASSEROLE

SERVES 8

5 or 6 squash, sliced
1 (10-ounce) can cream of mushroom soup
1/2 cup milk
1 (10-ounce) can asparagus spears
10 saltine crackers, crumbled
5 (or more) slices American cheese
1/2 cup (1 stick) margarine, cut into pieces
1 (3-ounce) can French-fried onions

Combine the squash with enough water to cover in a large saucepan. Bring to a boil. Boil until tender; drain. Combine the soup and the milk in a bowl and mix well. Layer one-half of the squash, one-half of the asparagus, the crackers and two or more slices of cheese in a 1 1/2-quart baking dish. Continue layering the remaining squash, the remaining asparagus, the soup mixture and three or more slices cheese. Dot with the margarine. Bake at 350 degrees for 20 minutes. Sprinkle the French-fried onions over the top. Bake for 10 minutes.

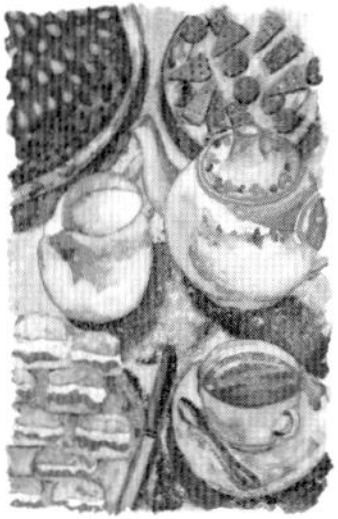

Jill Meeker

WHISKEY CAKE

SERVES 16

1 (2-layer) package butter recipe yellow cake mix
1 (4-ounce) package vanilla instant pudding mix
4 eggs, lightly beaten
1 cup milk
1/2 cup vegetable oil
1/4 cup whiskey
1 cup chopped pecans
1/2 cup (1 stick) butter
1 cup sugar
2/3 cup whiskey

Combine the cake mix, pudding mix, eggs, milk, oil and 1/4 cup whiskey in a mixing bowl and beat at medium speed for 3 minutes or until smooth and fluffy. Stir in the pecans. Spoon into a greased and floured tube pan. Bake at 350 degrees for 50 to 60 minutes. Combine the butter, sugar and 2/3 cup whiskey in a saucepan 5 minutes before the cake is done. Cook over low heat until the sugar dissolves, stirring frequently. Pour one-half of the syrup evenly over the hot cake. Let stand for 15 to 20 minutes. Invert the cake onto a rack or cake plate and pour the remaining syrup over the cake.

INTERNATIONAL FARE

Maria Solomon

STROMBOLI

SERVES 6 TO 8

A sandwich that melts in your mouth with homemade taste, this is an easy party favorite.

2 loaves frozen bread dough
8 ounces mushrooms, sliced
Butter for sautéing
1 pound ham, thinly sliced
12 ounces hard salami, thinly sliced
16 ounces provolone cheese, sliced
12 ounces mozzarella cheese, sliced
1 onion, thinly sliced
Oregano to taste
Basil to taste

Let the dough stand at room temperature for 2 hours or until thawed. Pat each loaf of dough into a 6×12-inch rectangle. Sauté the mushrooms in butter in a skillet until tender; drain. Layer the ham, salami, cheeses, onion and mushrooms lengthwise down the center of each rectangle. Sprinkle with oregano and basil. Fold the dough together to meet in the center. Pinch the sides and seams together, sealing completely. Place on an ungreased baking sheet. Bake at 375 degrees for 25 minutes. Slice and serve immediately.

Elizabeth Terrell

CHICKEN MARSALA

SERVES 4

No matter the get-together, this is a recipe that will get rave reviews. Accompany this dish with a salad and some homemade bread and it will be a perfect meal to take to a neighbor, someone who is sick, or someone with a new arrival.

12 ounces mushrooms, sliced
2 tablespoons butter
4 garlic cloves, minced
1 1/2 tablespoons lemon juice
1 pound boneless skinless chicken breasts
1/4 cup all-purpose flour
1/2 teaspoon salt
1/2 teaspoon pepper
2 tablespoons butter
1 tablespoon olive oil
3/4 cup marsala wine
1 teaspoon beef bouillon granules
1 tablespoon parsley
Hot cooked angel hair pasta

Sauté the mushrooms in 2 tablespoons butter in a large skillet until tender. Stir in the garlic and lemon juice. Remove the mushroom mixture to a bowl with a slotted spoon and set aside. Pound the chicken between sheets of waxed paper with a meat mallet until flattened. Cut the chicken into 1 1/2-inch-wide strips.

Combine the flour, salt and pepper in a bowl; mix well. Dredge the chicken in the seasoned flour, shaking off any excess. Add 2 tablespoons butter and the olive oil to the skillet and heat over medium-high heat until the butter is melted. Add the chicken and cook until brown and cooked through; cook in batches if necessary.

Remove the chicken to a plate with a slotted spoon. Add the wine and bouillon granules to the skillet. Cook until thickened, stirring constantly and scraping up any brown bits from the bottom of the skillet. Return the mushroom mixture and chicken to the skillet. Add the parsley and heat through. Serve over angel hair pasta.

Julie Hoffman

TIRAMISU

SERVES 8

Get ready for a party in your mouth—oh, just divine!
Tiramisu must mean "heaven" in Italian.

3 egg yolks
1/2 cup sugar
2 tablespoons Cognac or Kahlúa
1 cup brewed espresso or strong coffee
10 ounces mascarpone cheese, softened
3 egg whites
1/4 cup baking cocoa
20 (about) ladyfingers, toasted

Combine the egg yolks, sugar, Cognac, and 1 tablespoon of the espresso in a mixing bowl. Beat for 2 to 3 minutes or until foamy. Add the cheese and beat until smooth. Beat the egg whites in a mixing bowl until stiff peaks form. Fold into the cheese mixture. Dip the ladyfingers in the remaining espresso. Layer the ladyfingers, cheese mixture and baking cocoa one-third at a time in a glass serving bowl or dish. Chill, covered, until serving time. Spoon into individual dessert dishes.

Susan Rowe

MEXICAN CORN BREAD CASSEROLE

SERVES 6 TO 8

No Mexican night will be without this recipe once you make it the first time.

- 1 pound ground beef
- 1 onion, chopped
- 3 jalapeño chiles, seeded and chopped (optional)
- 3 eggs, lightly beaten
- 1 1/2 cups self-rising cornmeal
- 1 cup cream-style corn
- 1 cup buttermilk
- 2/3 cup vegetable oil
- 1/2 cup medium picante sauce
- 1 teaspoon salt
- 1 1/2 to 2 cups (6 to 8 ounces) shredded sharp Cheddar cheese

Brown the ground beef in a skillet, stirring until crumbly; drain. Combine ground beef, onion, jalapeño chiles, eggs, cornmeal, corn, buttermilk, oil, picante sauce and salt in a bowl; mix well. Layer the batter and cheese one-half at a time in a greased 9×12-inch or 3-quart baking dish. Bake at 350 degrees for 1 hour. Serve with additional cheese, salsa and sour cream.

Lisa Jennings

ENCHILADA CASSEROLE

SERVES 8

A filling dish that serves well the next night, so you can make it ahead of time. Great for busy school schedules!

1 envelope enchilada sauce mix
1 (6-ounce) can tomato paste
3/4 cup water
1 1/2 pounds ground beef
1 teaspoon garlic salt
1/2 teaspoon onion powder
1 (16-ounce) can refried beans
1 (10-ounce) package flour tortillas
1 1/2 cups (6 ounces) shredded Cheddar cheese
1 1/2 cups (6 ounces) shredded Monterey Jack cheese

Prepare the enchilada sauce mix according to the package directions, substituting the tomato paste and water for the tomato sauce. Brown the ground beef with the garlic salt and onion powder in a skillet, stirring until the ground beef is crumbly; drain. Stir in the refried beans and 1/2 cup of the prepared enchilada sauce.

Cover the bottom of a 9×13-inch baking dish with one-third of the tortillas dipped in the remaining sauce. Layer half the ground beef mixture, half the Cheddar cheese, half the Monterey Jack cheese and one-third of the tortillas in the baking dish. Continue layering with the remaining ground beef mixture, the remaining tortillas, the remaining sauce, the remaining Cheddar cheese and the remaining Monterey Jack cheese. Bake, covered, at 375 degrees for 20 minutes. Let stand for 5 minutes before serving. Serve with shredded lettuce, chopped cilantro, diced tomatoes, avocado slices and homemade pico de gallo.

You can substitute 3 cups of shredded cooked chicken for the ground beef.

Maria Solomon

FROZEN MARGARITA PIE

SERVES 6

Calling all margarita lovers: this pie is a refreshing end to any summer get-together.

1 1/4 cups finely crushed pretzels
1/2 cup (1 stick) butter, melted
1/4 cup sugar
1 (14-ounce) can sweetened condensed milk
1/3 cup lime juice from concentrate
3 to 4 tablespoons tequila
2 to 3 tablespoons Triple Sec
1 cup whipped cream

Combine the pretzels, butter and sugar in a bowl; mix well. Press firmly and evenly over the bottom and up the side of a 9-inch pie plate. Combine the condensed milk, lime juice, tequila and Triple Sec in a large bowl; blend until smooth. Fold in the whipped cream. Pour into the prepared pie shell. Garnish the top with lime twists, lime slices, pretzels or a mixture of orange zest and sugar. Freeze, covered, for 2 hours or until set.

SANGRIA

SERVES 8 TO 10

A fruity mixture of wine and Triple Sec that pairs well with guacamole and tortilla chips.

1.5 liters Burgundy wine
1 fifth of Triple Sec
1 to 2 cups orange juice, or more to taste
2 to 3 teaspoons sugar, or more to taste
Apple slices
Orange slices

Divide the wine and Triple Sec between two large pitchers. Stir equal amounts of the orange juice and sugar into each pitcher. Add apple and orange slices. Chill, covered, for 8 hours. Add additional orange juice and sugar if needed. Serve over ice.

TAILGATING

Joan Grubbs

"TIGER" PARTY DIP

SERVES 16 TO 18

Serve this creamy dip with vegetables, or your favorite crackers, to please any tailgater.

16 ounces cream cheese, softened
1/2 cup Miracle Whip salad dressing
1/3 cup freshly grated Parmesan cheese
10 slices bacon, crisp-cooked and crumbled
1/4 cup sliced green onions

Combine the cream cheese and salad dressing in a bowl and blend until smooth. Add the Parmesan cheese, bacon and green onions; mix well. Chill, covered, until serving time.

Pat Distel

"ROLL TIDE" GOURMET CHILI

SERVES 8 TO 10

This tailgate favorite can be made ahead of time.

2 pounds ground round
1 large onion, chopped
1 green bell pepper, chopped
1 cup chopped celery
2/3 stick butter
1 (20-ounce) can crushed tomatoes
1 (16-ounce) can tomato sauce
1 cup water
3 garlic cloves, mashed
3 tablespoons chili powder
1 teaspoon each oregano, salt and pepper
1 teaspoon hot red pepper sauce
2 (15-ounce) cans kidney beans, drained and rinsed

Brown the ground round in a skillet, stirring until crumbly; drain. Sauté the onion, bell pepper and celery in the butter in a skillet until tender. Add the beef, tomatoes, tomato sauce, water, garlic, chili powder, oregano, salt, pepper and hot sauce; mix well. Simmer for 2 hours. Stir in the beans. Simmer for 1 hour, stirring occasionally.

Esther White

"REBEL" CHEESY BEER BREAD

SERVES 12

Hey, you don't have to just drink beer; you can eat it, too.

3 cups self-rising flour
1 (12-ounce) bottle beer
1 cup (4 ounces) shredded sharp Cheddar cheese
3 tablespoons sugar
1 teaspoon garlic powder (optional)

Combine the flour, beer, cheese, sugar and garlic powder in a large bowl; mix well. Pour into a well-greased loaf pan. Bake at 350 degrees for 45 to 60 minutes or until golden brown.

Nora Fern Truby and Brittney York

"GATOR" POTATO CHIP COOKIES

MAKES ABOUT 6 DOZEN

No need to have dip out for these chips!

3 cups all-purpose flour
$1\frac{1}{2}$ cups crushed potato chips
$1\frac{1}{2}$ cups (3 sticks) margarine, softened
$1\frac{1}{2}$ cups sugar
1 cup chopped walnuts
2 egg yolks, lightly beaten
1 teaspoon baking soda
1 teaspoon vanilla extract

Combine the flour, potato chips, margarine, sugar, walnuts, egg yolks, baking soda and vanilla in a bowl; mix well. Shape into balls and place on a greased cookie sheet. Flatten with a fork. Bake at 375 degrees for 12 minutes.

Olivia Grubbs

"BULLDOG" BRITTLE

MAKES 3 TO 4 DOZEN

A simple recipe that makes a great treat and is easy to transport. This is a great recipe for children to help with.

Whole or broken graham crackers
1 to 1 1/2 cups chopped pecans or other favorite nuts
1/2 cup (1 stick) butter
1/2 cup (1 stick) margarine
1/2 cup sugar

Line a baking sheet with foil or baking parchment. Arrange the graham crackers in a single layer, covering the lined baking sheet. Sprinkle evenly with the pecans. Melt the butter and margarine in a saucepan. Stir in the sugar. Bring to a boil and boil for no longer than 2 minutes. Pour evenly over the pecans. Bake at 350 degrees for 12 to 15 minutes. Let stand until completely cool. Break into pieces.

TEA PARTY

Julie Knott

CRAB PUFFS

MAKES 4 DOZEN

This is an easy treat that you can do ahead of time. Garnish each puff with a sprig of parsley, if desired.

6 ounces crab meat
1 (6-ounce) jar Old English cheese spread
2 tablespoons mayonnaise
1/2 cup (1 stick) butter, softened
1/2 teaspoon salt
1/2 teaspoon seasoned salt
1/2 teaspoon garlic powder
6 English muffins, split and cut into quarters

Combine the crab meat, cheese spread, mayonnaise, butter, salt, seasoned salt and garlic powder in a bowl; mix well. Spread the crab meat mixture on each English muffin piece and place on a baking sheet. Bake at 350 degrees for 20 minutes.

These freeze well. Assemble and freeze, covered, on a baking sheet. Transfer to sealable plastic freezer bags and store in the freezer until baking time. Bake as directed.

Robyn Ridgeway

FANTASTIC CHICKEN SALAD

SERVES 10 TO 12

A wedding shower or baby shower isn't complete without this delicious salad. For a unique presentation, serve with whole grain crackers or small pieces of bread on a bird's nest of mixed greens.

5 or 6 boneless skinless chicken breasts
Salt and pepper to taste
3 tablespoons lemon juice
3 hard-cooked eggs
1 rib celery, finely chopped
1 cup mayonnaise
1 cup green grapes, cut into halves
1/2 cup slivered almonds, toasted
1/4 teaspoon celery salt
Lettuce

Cook the chicken in enough salted and peppered boiling water to cover in a large saucepan until cooked through. Drain, discarding the cooking liquid. Let the chicken stand until cool. Finely chop the chicken and toss with the lemon juice in a bowl to coat. Chill, covered, for 3 to 10 hours or until serving time. Stir in the eggs, celery, mayonnaise, grapes, almonds and celery salt. Season with salt and pepper as needed. Serve on a bed of lettuce.

Glenda Pope

GLENDA'S BISCUITS

MAKES APPROXIMATELY 10 TO 15

No Southern ham should be anywhere else. Add butter and a slice of garden fresh tomato to warm biscuits and close your eyes!

2 cups butter-flavor shortening
4 cups self-rising flour
1 cup buttermilk

Cut the shortening into the flour in a large bowl until crumbly. Add the buttermilk and mix well. Pat 1/2 inch thick on a lightly floured surface. Cut with a biscuit cutter and place on a baking sheet. Bake at 475 degrees for 10 minutes or until golden brown.

Pat Kennedy

BLUEBERRY CRUNCH

SERVES 10

Serve right out of the oven à la mode, mmmm.

1 (20-ounce) can crushed pineapple
3 cups blueberries
3/4 cup sugar
1 (2-layer) package lemon cake mix
1/2 cup (1 stick) butter
1 cup chopped pecans

Layer the pineapple, blueberries, sugar and cake mix in a 9×13-inch baking dish. Dot with the butter and sprinkle with the pecans. Bake at 350 degrees for 45 minutes.

Kristy Thorstad

CITRUS TEA

MAKES 5 CUPS

A refreshing spring and summertime drink that will complement any front porch rocker.

3 cups water
2 cloves
1 family-size tea bag
2/3 cup sugar
1 1/2 cups pineapple juice
1/2 cup orange juice
2 to 4 tablespoons fresh lemon juice

Combine the water and cloves in a saucepan and bring to a boil. Boil for 10 minutes. Remove from the heat and add the tea bag. Let stand to steep for 10 minutes. Remove and discard the tea bag and cloves. Stir the sugar, pineapple juice, orange juice and lemon juice into the tea. Chill for 2 to 10 hours.

THE BIG EASY

Teresa Ward

JAMBALAYA

SERVES 8 TO 10

1 pound smoked sausage, sliced
8 ounces deli ham, chopped
1/4 cup (1/2 stick) butter, melted
2 onions, chopped
1 small bell pepper, chopped
1/4 cup minced garlic
1 (16-ounce) can chopped tomatoes
1/4 cup all-purpose flour
32 ounces chicken broth or beef broth
4 or 5 bay leaves
1/2 teaspoon thyme
10 to 12 dashes of hot red pepper sauce
Salt to taste
3 to 4 pounds peeled shrimp
2 or 3 chicken breasts, cooked and chopped
2 cups rice
Green onions, chopped

Brown the sausage and ham in the butter in a large saucepan. Add the onions, bell pepper and garlic. Cook until tender. Stir in the undrained tomatoes and flour. Cook until thickened, stirring constantly. Add the broth, bay leaves, thyme and hot sauce. Season with salt. Add the shrimp, chicken and rice. Cook over low heat until the rice is tender and the moisture has been absorbed, stirring frequently. Remove the bay leaves. Sprinkle with green onions.

Jennifer Lichty

SHRIMP ÉTOUFFEE

SERVES 4 TO 6

Your kitchen will smell like the gourmet chef you can be, and the family won't want you to take this dish away to the church social.

1/4 cup (1/2 stick) butter
1/3 cup all-purpose flour
4 teaspoons minced garlic
1/3 cup chopped celery
3 green onions, sliced
1 3/4 cups water
1 1/2 pounds medium shrimp, peeled and deveined
2 tablespoons chopped parsley
1 teaspoon salt
Cayenne pepper to taste
Hot cooked jasmine rice

Melt the butter in a large saucepan over medium heat. Add the flour gradually and cook until light golden brown, stirring constantly. Add the garlic and cook for 1 minute, stirring constantly. Add the celery, green onions and 1/4 cup of the water. Cook until the celery is tender.

Add the remaining 1 1/2 cups water, the shrimp and parsley. Bring to a boil over medium-high heat, stirring constantly. Cover and simmer over low heat for 15 minutes. Season with the salt and cayenne pepper. Simmer, uncovered, for 5 minutes, stirring occasionally and adding additional water as needed for a thinner consistency. Serve over rice.

Michelle Ward

JALAPENO CHEESE GRITS CASSEROLE

SERVES 6 TO 8

4 cups water
1/2 teaspoon salt
1 cup quick-cooking grits
1 cup (4 ounces) shredded sharp Cheddar cheese
8 ounces processed cheese with jalapeño chiles, cut into cubes
1/4 cup (1/2 stick) butter
3 eggs, beaten
2 tablespoons chopped jalapeño chiles
1 tablespoon Worcestershire sauce
Paprika to taste

Combine the water and salt in a saucepan and bring to a boil. Stir in the grits. Cook, covered, over low heat for 5 minutes, stirring occasionally. Remove from the heat. Add the Cheddar cheese, processed cheese and butter and stir until melted. Stir in the eggs, jalapeño chiles and Worcestershire sauce. Pour into a greased 2-quart baking dish. Sprinkle with paprika. Bake at 350 degrees for 40 to 45 minutes or until set. Let stand for 10 minutes before serving.

Pat Distel

BANANA-NUT LAYER CAKE

SERVES 12

- 2/3 cup shortening
- 1 2/3 cups sugar
- 3 eggs
- 2/3 cup buttermilk
- 2 1/4 cups cake flour
- 1 1/4 teaspoons baking powder
- 1 1/4 teaspoons baking soda
- 1 teaspoon salt
- 1 1/4 cups mashed bananas
- 2/3 cup finely chopped pecans or walnuts
- 1/2 cup (1 stick) butter, softened
- 8 ounces cream cheese, softened
- 1 (1-pound) package confectioners' sugar
- 2 teaspoons vanilla extract
- 1 cup chopped pecans
- 1 cup flaked coconut

Beat the first ten ingredients in a large mixing bowl for 30 seconds at low speed, scraping the bowl constantly. Beat at high speed for 3 minutes. Pour into two 9-inch cake pans. Bake at 350 degrees for 30 to 40 minutes or until the cake tests done. Cool on a wire rack. Beat the butter, cream cheese, confectioners' sugar and vanilla in a bowl until light and creamy. Stir in 1 cup pecans and the coconut. Spread between the layers and over the top and side of the cake.

Old Favorites

A selection from *A Taste of Georgia* and *A Taste of Georgia, Another Serving*

Tricia Slomka, A Taste of Georgia, Another Serving

SAUSAGE STUFFED MUSHROOMS

1 pound mushroom caps
1/4 cup (1/2 stick) butter
1 pound bulk pork sausage
8 ounces cream cheese, softened
Grated Parmesan cheese

Sauté the mushrooms in the butter in a skillet until tender. Let stand to cool slightly. Arrange stem side up in a single layer. Brown the sausage in a skillet, stirring until crumbly; drain. Combine the sausage and cream cheese in a bowl; mix well. Spoon into the mushroom caps. Place on a baking sheet and sprinkle with Parmesan cheese. Bake at 350 degrees for 10 minutes or until heated through.

May be made a day ahead and chilled until baking time.

Pam Lee and Mary Ann Reese, A Taste of Georgia

CHEESE RICE KRISPIES

MAKES 5 DOZEN

$1^1/_2$ cups (3 sticks) margarine, softened
8 to 10 ounces sharp cheese, shredded
2 cups all-purpose flour or self-rising flour
Dash of ground red pepper
$2^1/_4$ to $2^1/_2$ cups Rice Krispies cereal

Combine the margarine and cheese in a bowl; mix well. Add the flour and red pepper; mix well. Fold in the cereal. Shape the mixture into small balls and place on a greased cookie sheet. Bake at 375 degrees for 10 to 15 minutes.

Jewell Meltzer, A Taste of Georgia, Another Serving

VIDALIA ONION-TOMATO SALAD

SERVES 5 TO 6

1 jumbo Vidalia onion, sliced into thin rings and separated
4 tomatoes, peeled and sliced
1/4 teaspoon chopped fresh or dried herbs (parsley, chives, basil and dill weed)
Celery salt to taste
Salt and pepper to taste

3/4 cup olive oil, or 1/4 cup olive oil and 1/2 cup corn, safflower or soy oil
1 cup wine vinegar
1 teaspoon Dijon mustard
1/2 teaspoon dry mustard
1/4 teaspoon sugar
1/2 teaspoon salt, or to taste

Layer the onion, tomatoes, herbs, celery salt and salt and pepper to taste in a 9×13-inch pan or large bowl. Chill, covered, for 3 hours. Combine the olive oil, vinegar, Dijon mustard, dry mustard, sugar and 1/2 teaspoon salt in a jar with a tight-fitting lid. Season with pepper. Secure the lid and shake to combine. Drizzle to taste over the salad. Chill any unused dressing. If possible, bring the dressing to room temperature before serving.

Helen Abraham, A Taste of Georgia, Another Serving

IMPOSSIBLE GARDEN PIE

SERVES 6

An easy, light meal.

2 cups zucchini, quartered and sliced
$1^1/2$ cups chopped tomatoes
$^1/2$ cup chopped onion
$^1/2$ cup (2 ounces) grated Parmesan cheese
$^1/4$ teaspoon pepper
$1^1/2$ cups skim milk
$^3/4$ cup baking mix
3 eggs, lightly beaten

Layer the zucchini, tomatoes, onion and cheese in a lightly greased 7×11-inch baking dish. Sprinkle with the pepper. Combine the skim milk, baking mix and eggs in a mixing bowl. Beat for 1 minute or until smooth. Pour evenly over the prepared layers. Bake at 400 degrees for 30 minutes. Let stand for 5 minutes before slicing.

Teresa Lovett, A Taste of Georgia

CHICKEN AND DRESSING CASSEROLE

SERVES 6 TO 8

Good and easy!

1/4 cup (1/2 stick) margarine, melted
1/2 (10-ounce) can cream of celery soup
1/2 (10-ounce) can cream of chicken soup
1/2 (12-ounce) can evaporated milk, or 1 1/2 cups milk
1 package corn bread stuffing mix
1 1/2 cups chicken broth
2 pounds boiled chicken, chopped

Combine the margarine, cream of celery soup, cream of chicken soup and evaporated milk in a bowl; mix well. Combine the stuffing mix with the chicken broth in a bowl; mix well. Layer the chicken, soup mixture and stuffing mixture in a 2-quart baking dish. Bake at 425 degrees for 25 minutes or until brown.

Marie Umbach, A Taste of Georgia

SOUR CREAM BREAKFAST CAKE

SERVES 16

- 1/2 cup (1 stick) butter or margarine, softened
- 1 cup sugar
- 1 cup sour cream
- 2 eggs
- 2 cups all-purpose flour
- 1 teaspoon baking powder
- 1 teaspoon baking soda
- 1 teaspoon vanilla extract
- 1/2 cup packed brown sugar
- 1 teaspoon cinnamon
- 1/4 cup chopped nuts

Cream the butter and sugar in a mixing bowl. Add the sour cream and eggs. Beat until light and fluffy. Add the flour, baking powder, baking soda and vanilla. Beat until smooth. Combine the brown sugar, cinnamon and nuts in a bowl; mix well. Layer the batter and nut mixture one-half at a time in a greased bundt pan. Bake at 350 degrees for 45 minutes. Cool in the pan for 10 minutes.

Index

To order more copies of this cookbook
or our other award-winning cookbooks, *A Taste of Georgia*
and *A Taste of Georgia, Another Serving*,
visit us at www.newnanjuniorserviceleague.org
or call (770) 251-0113.